A BEACON · BIOGRAPHY

Stephen Colbert

Tamra B. Orr

PURPLE TOAD
PUBLISHING

Copyright © 2018 by Purple Toad Publishing, Inc. All rights reserved. No part of this book may be reproduced without written permission from the publisher. Printed and bound in the United States of America.

Printing   1   2   3   4   5   6   7   8   9

A Beacon Biography

Angelina Jolie
Anthony Davis
Big Time Rush
Bill Nye
Cam Newton
Carly Rae Jepsen
Carson Wentz
Chadwick Boseman
Daisy Ridley
Drake
Ed Sheeran
Ellen DeGeneres
Elon Musk
Ezekiel Elliott
Gal Gadot
Harry Styles of One Direction
Jennifer Lawrence

John Boyega
Kevin Durant
Lorde
Malala
Maria von Trapp
Markus "Notch" Persson, Creator of Minecraft
Millie Bobby Brown
Misty Copeland
Mo'ne Davis
Muhammad Ali
Neil deGrasse Tyson
Peyton Manning
Robert Griffin III (RG3)
Stephen Colbert
Stephen Curry
Tom Holland
Zendaya

Publisher's Cataloging-in-Publication Data
Orr, Tamra B.
    Stephen Colbert / written by Tamra B. Orr.
      p. cm.
Includes bibliographic references, glossary, and index.
ISBN 9781624693915
1. Colbert, Stephen, 1964—Juvenile literature. 2. Comedians—United States—Biography—Juvenile literature. 3. Television personalities—United States—Biography—Juvenile literature. I. Series: Beacon biography.
  PN2287.C5695 2017
  792.76092

Library of Congress Control Number: 2017956829

eBook ISBN: 9781624693922

ABOUT THE AUTHOR: Tamra B. Orr is a full-time author living in the Pacific Northwest with her family. She graduated from Ball State University in Muncie, Indiana. She has written more than 500 books about everything from historical events and career choices to controversial issues and celebrity biographies. On those rare occasions that she is not writing a book, she is reading one. She stays up extra late every weeknight in order to watch *The Late Show with Stephen Colbert*. If she cannot keep her eyes open, she records the episode because she knows Colbert will always make her laugh.

PUBLISHER'S NOTE: This story has not been authorized or endorsed by Stephen Colbert.

CONTENTS

Chapter

1

The C.O.L.B.E.R.T.

It was the moment Stephen Colbert (*kohl-BAYR*) had been looking forward to for weeks. He could not keep the smile off his face as he welcomed *The Colbert Report*'s first guest of the evening, astronaut Sunita "Suni" Williams. She was there to announce the name of the International Space Station's (ISS) new node, or room. The other rooms were known as Unity, Harmony, and Destiny.

Earlier in 2009, NASA had sponsored a contest on what to name the new room. NASA liked the name Serenity. More than one million people from all across the country submitted their votes for the best name. Legacy, Earthwise, and Venture were high on the list. The winning name, however, with 230,539 of the 1.1 million votes, was . . . Colbert. Stephen Colbert had asked his viewers to vote for his name. They listened! But when astronaut Williams came on the show, April 14, 2009, she had some disappointing news. The new ISS module would be named Tranquility, after the Sea of Tranquility, where *Apollo 11* had landed on the moon in 1969.

Astronaut Suni Williams used the C.O.L.B.E.R.T. treadmill quite often while living on the International Space Station.

The audience groaned. Colbert's smile faltered. Then Williams added the good news. "Your name will be in space, in a very important place," she reassured the comedian. Instead of being the name of the node, his name would be on the ISS's new treadmill. It would be the Combined Operational Load Bearing External Resistance Treadmill, or the C.O.L.B.E.R.T. Colbert's smile—and jokes—came back. "I think a treadmill is better than a node because the node is just a box for the treadmill," he said. "Nobody says, 'Hey, my mom bought me a Nike box.' They want the shoes that are inside."

While it might seem strange to have a treadmill on the ISS, this equipment helps astronauts stay healthy. The crew keeps their muscles and bones stronger by exercising for hours every day. Of course, running in space is not easy. Astronauts have to wear elastic straps on their shoulders and around their waists to keep them from shooting off the treadmill. The treadmill cannot risk shaking the ISS with its vibrations, either. That could disturb some of the science experiments or confuse the onboard computers. The C.O.L.B.E.R.T. was specially built on springs and a strong base so that it would not rattle the ISS.

NASA was grateful to Stephen Colbert for telling his fans about the contest. NASA's Bill Gerstenmaier, who is in charge of human exploration, told *The Atlantic*, "This spread overall awareness of the International Space Station." Curt Wiederhoeft, part of the team that built the treadmill, added, "I think it's great that Mr. Colbert got his audience interested in the space station. Comedy Central attracts a lot of younger viewers, and the space program's going to need the next generation's support and interest."

The ISS treadmill contest was not Colbert's first attempt at getting his name put on something. In 2006, Hungary held a contest for naming one of its bridges. Although Colbert's name was the top one, Hungary's government said it would not work. Why? Because it had to be named for someone who was Hungarian—and dead! One American airline has a plane named *Air Colbert*. Ben & Jerry's has an ice cream flavor called Stephen Colbert's Americone Dream®. Amazingly, there are even several insect species, plus a few spiders, that have been named after Colbert.

Who is the man who has so many fans? He is an actor, author, comedian, and talk show host. He is also a husband, father, and Sunday school teacher. Long before stardom, however, he had to go through one of life's biggest challenges.

*The **Air Colbert**. Imagine having a plane, a treadmill, an ice cream flavor, and even insects and spiders with your name!*

Tennessee

North Carolina

South Carolina

Georgia

James Island,
Charleston

Alabama

Florida

Colbert's life began on the east coast of South Carolina.

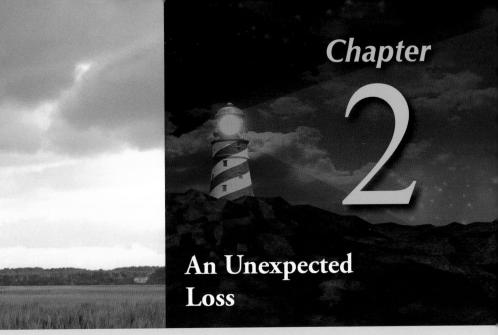
An Unexpected Loss

When Stephen Tyrone Colbert was born on May 13, 1964, he joined a huge family. His father, James, was the dean of a medical school. His mother, Lorna, stayed at home in order to take care of Stephen—and his 10 brothers and sisters: Elizabeth, Peter, Paul, William, Mary, Thomas, Edward, Jay, Margo, and James. The Catholic family lived on James Island in Charleston, South Carolina. Life was loud and busy—but happy.

Everything changed on September 11, 1974. Brothers Paul and Peter, along with their father, were flying to Connecticut to check out a private school when the unthinkable happened. Eastern Airline Flight 212 crashed in a North Carolina cornfield. No one survived the disaster.

At home, most of the siblings were either living on their own or off at school. "I was left alone a lot after Dad and the boys died . . . and it was just me and Mom for a long time," Colbert recalled in an interview with *GQ*. He said he coped with the loss by watching his mother. "And by her example I am not bitter," he said. "By *her* example. She was not. Broken, yes. Bitter, no."

Colbert learned to accept what had happened to his family. "Acceptance is not defeat. Acceptance is just awareness," he explained to *GQ*. "Boy, did I

By the time Colbert was in high school, he had developed an attitude that sometimes got him in trouble.

have a bomb when I was 10. That was quite an explosion. And I learned to love it. . . . I love the thing that I most wish had not happened. You can't change everything about the world," he added. "You certainly can't change things that have already occurred."

In an interview with *Entertainment Weekly*, Colbert talked about how he dealt with his grief. "The interesting thing about grief, I think, is that it is its own size," he said. "And grief comes to you. . . . Grief is its own thing. . . . If you try to ignore it, it will be like a wolf at your door."

After the plane crash, Stephen and his mother moved into downtown Charleston. Stephen was sent to Porter-Gaud prep school. He was far from a good student there. "There was no way to threaten me," he told *GQ*. "It was like, '*What?* What's that? Oh, okay, I might get a *bad grade*? Oh no. Wouldn't want that?'"

Instead, Stephen spent most of his time reading as many books as he could. His absolute favorites were the *Lord of the Rings* (LOTR) series by J.R.R. Tolkien. He discovered the books when he was thirteen years old. How thrilled he would have been to know that one day, he and his entire family would have small parts in an LOTR movie. They all appeared in the Lake-town sequence in the film *The Hobbit: The Desolation of Smaug*.

Colbert told reporter Eric Spitznagel that he loved science fiction because it helped him escape. "I think there's absolute truth in escaping the reality of your present predicament. . . . It doesn't have to be tragedy. There's a tragedy to being thirteen. Things are changing. Friends are changing. Your body is changing. You need to escape that."

"I had so many books taken away from me," he told *GQ*'s Joel Lovell. "I read a book a day. Spent all of my allowance on books. Every birthday, confirmation, Christmas—books, please, stacks of books." He was also a great fan of the role-playing game Dungeons and Dragons and played it for hours with his friends.

While Stephen was busy reading and playing games, he was also watching many different television shows—especially news anchors and talk show hosts. Since he was from South Carolina, he had a strong Southern accent. He wanted to get rid of it because he wanted to sound more like a news announcer. "I wanted to seem smart," he told *60 Minutes* in 2006.

Stephen was not sure what he wanted to do when he grew up. He had thought about a career in marine biology, but that was impossible. When he was young, he had surgery to fix a burst eardrum. The operation injured his inner ear so badly that most of it had to be removed. This left Colbert deaf on one side. He was also told not to put his head underwater.

The idea of acting for a living was not one he gave much thought to, but his mother was a great role model. "My mother always loved acting and taught us kids how to do falls," he told Spitznagel. "She would be in the kitchen and she'd suddenly just faint in a swoon, put a hand to her forehead and fall backward. . . . She would teach us to do the roll-down so you wouldn't hurt yourself as you fell. 'Remember, it's ankle, knee, hip, chest, arm, head.' We all learned how to do the falls. And we'd fall all over the house, all the time, and my mom was fine with it. I guess that love for all things theatrical just rubbed off on me."

Lorna Colbert

Little did he know those words would follow him into college—and far beyond.

At Northwestern University, Colbert starred with many talented students, including David Schwimmer (second row, second from left).

From Philosophy to Improv

When Colbert went to college in 1982, he quickly discovered that even the best of plans can be derailed. At Hampden-Sydney College in Virginia, Colbert decided to study philosophy. To have a little fun, he joined the school's theater group. Suddenly, he knew what he wanted from life. He left Hampden-Sydney in his junior year and transferred to Northwestern University in Evanston, Illinois. Northwestern is known for its theater program. Some of its famous graduates include actors Zach Braff, Zooey Deschanel, and Julia Louis-Dreyfus.

Colbert worked long and hard at Northwestern, completing his three-year program in two years. He also worked two jobs. One was in the college's cafeteria. One was in the library. "I was just pushing myself too hard," he told *Northwestern Magazine*. "I weighed about as much as a kitten." Although he started out thinking he would be a serious actor, he was drawn to comedy—and improv. In improv (IM-präv), actors do not have a script to follow. Instead they make up jokes and skits as they go along. It requires very fast thinking.

When actor David Schwimmer came on Colbert's show in early 2016, the two men discussed the fun they had together at Northwestern. They were in

Colbert at Northwestern in 1984

an improv group called the No Fun Mud Piranhas. Schwimmer said, "Steve, I could never keep up with him. Your mind is just so ridiculously fast. I actually was really grateful for being in that group with you because I realized that's why I can't do that."

Colbert graduated from Northwestern in 1986 with a degree in theater. He spent most of his time practicing improv and comedy. He also appeared on commercials and was a guest on the popular improv series *Whose Line Is It Anyway?* He did stories for the news show *Good Morning America.* And he worked with the comedy group The Second City in Chicago.

While Colbert was building his career, he was also creating a family. In 1993, he married Evelyn McGee. He

In 1993, Colbert (third from left), along with friend and actor Steve Carrell (left), were part of the comedy group The Second City.

Colbert and his wife, Evelyn, are good friends with fellow talk show host and comedian Jon Stewart and his wife, Tracey.

originally met her at a festival in Charleston. His mother had offered him an extra ticket, so he went. "I walked into the theater, and there across the lobby was my wife. I thought, Oh, wow, there's my wife," he told Spitznagel. He knew immediately that he was going to marry McGee. "There was never a doubt in my mind," he added.

In 1995, Colbert added "father" to his list of accomplishments when his daughter Madeleine was born. In 2011, he gave a speech to Northwestern University graduates. He compared life to his comedy style. He said, "Life is an improvisation. You have no idea what's going to happen next and you are mostly just making things up as you go along."

By the mid-1990s, Colbert was doing well. He had a family, and his career was growing steadily. Quite soon, it would soar—and the rest of the country would get to see the comedian on a daily basis.

Colbert helped bring the world's attention to the Comedy Central station. His funny, exaggerated portrayal of an American patriot talk-show host earned him and his show a Peabody award.

Comedy Central and His Own Show

In 1991, a new television channel was added to the cable lineup. Called Comedy Central, it was dedicated to making people laugh. It was a great place for Colbert, along with friends and classmates Amy Sedaris and Paul Dinello, to try out their first show, *Exit 57*. It did well, running for one season (1995–1996) and winning a number of awards.

When *Exit 57* ended, the team created a new show, *Strangers with Candy*. It ran for three seasons and in 2005 was turned into a full-length film. Colbert cowrote and starred in the film. He wrote for other comedy shows as well. For example, he wrote a number of jokes and skits for *The Dana Carvey Show*.

One of the most popular shows on Comedy Central was *The Daily Show*. It began in 1996 and was hosted by Craig Kilborn. The show is similar to a typical news program, only the stories are told with lots of humor. Called satire, these "news reports" use exaggeration, irony, and other types of humor to poke fun at and criticize politicians, celebrities, and other people or situations in the news. On *The Daily Show*, the first five minutes were spent reading "Headlines." That segment was followed by "Other News" and then a feature from a reporter in the field. The show was not all one-sided, however. It usually ended with Kilborn interviewing an actor, author, or other well-known person. Colbert began reporting for the show in 1997.

In 1999, Jon Stewart took over as host for *The Daily Show*, and Colbert stayed on. (Stewart remained the host through the summer of 2015, when he stepped down. Trevor Noah replaced him.) Under Stewart, *The Daily Show* became extremely popular. During his years working on the show, Colbert developed many strong opinions about politics and other important issues. His humorous reports were extremely popular with TV watchers. One of his favorite bits was doing a pretend ad for a show called *The Colbert Report*. Adding to the humor, he kept the "nearly French" pronunciation of his last name: *kohl-BAYR reh-POR*.

Colbert often interviewed important people on his show, including General Ray Odierno, the Commanding General of the Multi-National Force in Iraq, in 2010.

The show did not exist. However, people began calling in and asking about it. When was it on? How could they see it? Comedy Central realized the potential profits of Colbert's program. The network offered Colbert his own show, and the first episode aired October 17, 2005.

On *The Colbert Report*, Colbert pretended to be a very loud, sometimes offensive

The Colbert Report *included news stories from around the world—but they were told with a humorous twist.*

reporter named—Stephen Colbert. In this role, he yelled, was easily angered, and was even rude, as well as very funny. His satire gained him many followers. They were called Colbert Nation. When Colbert asked those fans to submit his names to contests, they were quick to do so.

Meanwhile, Colbert's family had grown. Peter was born in 1998, and John in 2002.

In several interviews, Colbert said that being in front of the camera all the time could be very frightening—especially when he was not doing well. "You gotta learn to love when you're failing," he told *GQ*. "The embracing of that, the discomfort of failing in front of an audience, leads you to penetrate through the fear that blinds you. Fear is the mind killer."

Part of his humor comes from learning to laugh at himself. "I like to do things that are publicly embarrassing, to feel the embarrassment touch me and sink into me and then be gone," he admitted to *GQ*. "I like getting on elevators and singing too loudly in that small space." Colbert compared that feeling to a vapor in the air. "I would do things like that and just breathe it

To interview the cast of The Hobbit: The Battle of the Five Armies, Colbert dressed up in the costume he wore when he appeared briefly in The Hobbit: The Desolation of Smaug.

in," he said. Then he would breathe out again and reassure himself. "Nope, can't kill me. This thing can't kill me," he stated.

It was a good thing that Colbert could stand up to people pointing, laughing, and even criticizing him. In 2006, he was invited to the White House Correspondents Dinner. At this event, the president invites members of the media to dinner and thanks them for their hard work.

It is the job of the media to point out both good things and bad about what the president is accomplishing. At this time in U.S. politics, as in most times, the president had a lot of support—and a lot of critics.

It was Colbert's job to make a speech that would make the audience laugh—especially if President George W. Bush was part of that audience. Colbert made a number of statements that were meant to be funny. At the same time, they were critical of the government. His performance sent shock waves through the country.

President Bush did not think much of it was funny, but by the next day, everyone knew who Stephen Colbert was. The video of his speech went viral. His cable show ratings soared. Suddenly, he found himself named one of the 100 Most Influential People in the world by *TIME* magazine.

The Colbert Report aired for nine years. By then, Stephen Colbert had added "author" to his long list of skills. He published his book *I Am America (And So Can You!)* in 2007. That same year he applied to run for president of his state of South Carolina. Not surprisingly, his application was denied. (The bid was clearly a joke.) But his popularity grew.

By 2012, Colbert had published other books: *America Again: Rebecoming the Greatness We Never Weren't,* and *I Am a Pole (And So Can You!).*

He was ready to move beyond *The Colbert Report* by the end of 2014. "One hundred and sixty shows a year is just . . . can't be done," he told *Northwestern Magazine.* "Early in this process, I started calling this place 'the joy machine.' Because if it's not a joy machine, it's just a machine. . . . You can get caught in the gears."

Colbert wanted to move on before he got caught in those gears. He found the perfect place.

Colbert's sense of humor has few limits. In this photo from a Colbert Report *sketch, he reports for basic combat training. Things don't go well when he asks the drill sergeant, "Can I get a bellman?"*

Today, Colbert's name is—literally—up in lights in New York City. People sign up online weeks ahead to get tickets to see his show live.

The late-night news circuit has always been extremely competitive. For decades, two shows vied for the top spot: *The Late Show* and *The Tonight Show*. Both programs boasted high-energy celebrity hosts. The gig was coveted, and only a few comedy legends held the spot of host. One of those legends was Johnny Carson, who hosted *The Tonight Show*. He was followed by Jay Leno. David Letterman hosted *Late Night* for 13 years, and then *The Late Show* for more than 20 years. He welcomed guests to the stage of the Ed Sullivan Theater in New York for thousands of episodes. When he announced that he was retiring at the end of 2014, the big question was: Who would take his place?

That answer came in the form of Stephen Colbert. After years of playing a character on his own show, he was ready to be himself for a change.

The Late Show with Stephen Colbert aired its first episode on September 8, 2015. In the beginning he struggled to impress fans that still missed Letterman and his style. On the first episode, Colbert gave a heartfelt tribute to Letterman. "So just for the record, I am not replacing David Letterman," he stated. "His creative legacy is a high pencil mark on a doorframe that we all have to measure ourselves against. But we will try to honor his achievement by doing the best show we can and, occasionally, making the network very mad at us." As time passed, Colbert gathered more and more viewers. When 2017 arrived, *The Late Show* was constantly rating highly, often tying or even doing better than *The Tonight Show*, which by this time was hosted by Jimmy Fallon.

Colbert has found fame and a worldwide forum, and he remains a religious man. From the time he was a young boy living in a big Catholic home and throughout his broadcasts, he has declared his faith. One of his strong beliefs is giving to those less fortunate. His spirit of giving is clear in his speeches and in his actions.

In 2007, when he broke his left wrist, he started a campaign on *The Colbert Report* to raise money with WristStrong bracelets. In a matter of months, he had earned $171,525 in donations from the wristbands. He had celebrities autograph his cast, and then he auctioned it off when the cast was removed, earning an additional $17,000. He gave all the money to the Yellow Ribbon Fund, a charity that helps injured service members and their families.

Since 2007, Colbert has also been active in the Donors Choose project. Donors Choose is an organization that lists the needs of classrooms

Colbert welcomes the chance to meet with fans—of any age.

Colbert continues to be close friends with John Oliver, a fellow talk show host and comedian from Comedy Central. Both of them are experts in keeping the world laughing.

throughout the country. Donors can look through the list and choose how to help these classrooms.

When he left *The Colbert Report*, Colbert auctioned off his desk and fireplace. They went for $800,000. He divided this money to pay for every classroom project in his home state. It funded almost 1,000 projects at more than 375 South Carolina schools.

Throughout the years, Colbert has continued to donate money to Donors Choose, plus he encourages many others, including his famous guests, to do so as well. He often receives thank you cards and letters from students. According to *CBS News*, one student's thank-you note read, "Dear Stephen Colbert, Thank you for donating. . . . We heard you have a TV show but it is too late for us to watch. Are you funny?" In a classic response, Colbert replied, "If I'm not, I'm in big trouble."

When Colbert was asked to give a speech to the 2011 graduating class of Northwestern University, he had many jokes and stories to share. However, near the end of his speech, his message turned serious. "In my experience, you will truly serve only what you love, because, as the prophet says, service is love made visible. If you love friends, you will serve your friends. If you love community, you will serve your community. If you love money, you will serve your money. And," he added, "if you love only yourself, you will serve only yourself, and you will have only yourself. So . . . try to love others and serve others, and hopefully find those who love and serve you in return."

It is good advice from a man who learned at an early age how to love, how to grieve, and how to make people laugh.

It is highly likely that Colbert will keep making people laugh—and help them make sense of the world—for many years to come.

1964   Stephen Colbert is born in Charleston, South Carolina, on May 13.

1982–1984 He attends Hampden-Sydney College in Virginia.

1986   He graduates from Northwestern University in Evanston, Illinois, with a degree in theater.

1993   Stephen and Evelyn McGee marry.

1995   Their daughter Madeleine is born.

1995–1996 Colbert writes and performs in the sketch show *Exit 57* for Comedy Central.

1997   He joins Comedy Central's *The Daily Show* as a correspondent.

1998   His son Peter is born.

2002   Another son, John, is born.

2005   *Strangers with Candy* is released; the first episode of *The Colbert Report* airs on October 17.

2006   Colbert appears at the White House Correspondents Dinner. *TIME* magazine names him one of the 100 Most Influential People of the Year.

2007   He runs for president of his home state of South Carolina. His book *I Am America (And So Can You!)* is published.

2009   A treadmill on the International Space Station is named the C.O.L.B.E.R.T. after him.

2010   Colbert wins a Grammy for Best Comedy Album, *A Colbert Christmas: The Greatest Gift of All.*

2012   His books *America Again: Re-becoming the Greatness We Never Weren't* and *I Am a Pole (And So Can You!)* are published. Once again, *TIME* magazine names him one of the 100 Most Influential People of the Year.

2014   *The Colbert Report* wraps up its last episode.

2015   The first episode of *The Late Show with Stephen Colbert* airs on September 8. His first guest is George Clooney.

2017   Colbert hosts the 69th Primetime Emmy Awards show. Colbert is one of many celebrities raising money and contributing to those in need from Hurricanes Harvey, Irma, and Maria.

Further Reading

Orr, Tamra B. *Ellen DeGeneres*. Purple Toad Publishing, 2017

Szumski, Bonnie. *Stephen Colbert (People in the News)*. Lucent Books, 2012.

On the Internet

Episodes and highlights from *The Late Show with Stephen Colbert* YouTube:
    https://www.youtube.com/channel/UCMtFAi84ehTSYSE9XoHefig

IMDb: Stephen Colbert
    http://www.imdb.com/name/nm0170306/

Information about CBS and access to episodes of *The Late Show*:
    http://www.cbs.com/shows/the-late-show-with-stephen-colbert/

Works Consulted

Cilizza, Chris. "This Is the Most Controversial Correspondents' Dinner Speech
    Ever. But Nobody Knew It at the Time." *The Washington Post*, April 25, 2015.
    https://www.washingtonpost.com/news/the-fix/wp/2015/04/24/this-is-the-
    most-controversial-speech-ever-at-the-correspondents-dinner-and-i-was-
    there/?utm_term=.d955faf6530b

Colbert. Stephen. "Colbert's Commencement Address." *Northwestern*, June 17,
    2011. http://www.northwestern.edu/newscenter/stories/2011/06/colbert-
    speech-text.html

Coyle, Jake. "NASA: Colbert Name on Treadmill, Not Room." *NBC News*, April 14,
    2009. http://www.nbcnews.com/id/30217550/ns/technology_and_science-
    space/t/nasa-colbert-name-treadmill-not-room/#.WaPeqj6GPX4

Davidson, Sean. "Stephen Colbert: 5 Little-Known Facts about the *Late Show*'s
    New Host." *CBC News*, September 8, 2015. http://www.cbc.ca/news/
    entertainment/stephen-colbert-late-show-5-facts-1.3215577

Garber, Megan. "Stephen Colbert: Comedian, Emmy Winner, Fitness Trainer to
    Astronauts." *The Atlantic*, September 23, 2013. https://www.theatlantic.com/
    technology/archive/2013/09/stephen-colbert-comedian-emmy-winner-fitness-
    trainer-to-astronauts/279897/

Kreps, Daniel. "Watch Stephen Colbert's David Letterman Tribute on 'Late Show.' "
    Rolling Stone, September 9, 2015. http://www.rollingstone.com/tv/news/
    watch-stephen-colberts-david-letterman-tribute-on-late-show-20150909

Lee, Rebecca. "Stephen Colbert Unveils Donors for #BestSchoolDay." *CBS News*,
    March 10, 2016. https://www.cbsnews.com/news/stephen-colbert-best-school-
    day-donors-choose-funding-american-classrooms-in-need/

Lovell, Joel. "The Late, Great Stephen Colbert." *GQ*, August 17, 2015. https://www.gq.com/story/stephen-colbert-gq-cover-story

Payne, Ed, et al. "NASA Name Cosmic Treadmill after Colbert." *CNN Entertainment*, April 15, 2009. http://www.cnn.com/2009/SHOWBIZ/TV/04/15/colbert.nasa/index.html

Phillips, Ian. "How Stephen Colbert Endured Tragedy and Became One of the Greatest Political Satirists of Our Time." *Business Insider*, September 16, 2015. http://www.businessinsider.com/stephen-colbert-bio-2015-9/#the-real-colbert-is-married-to-evelyn-mcgee-colbert-they-live-in-montclair-new-jersey-with-their-three-kids-23

Robinson, Joanna. "Stephen Colbert and His Entire Family Had Adorable Cameos in *The Hobbit: The Desolation of Smaug*." *Pajiba*, December 30, 2013. http://www.pajiba.com/miscellaneous/stephen-colbert-and-his-entire-family-had-adorable-cameos-in-the-hobbit-the-desolation-of-smaug.php#.U0wQk-bqdtA

Rome, Emily. "Stephen Colbert in *Playboy*: A Rare Serious Interview." *Entertainment Weekly*, October 16, 2012. http://ew.com/article/2012/10/16/stephen-colbert-real-playboy-interview/

Rowles, Dustin. "20 Remarkable Facts You Never Knew about Stephen Colbert." *Salon*, April 15, 2014. http://www.salon.com/2014/04/15/20_remarkable_facts_you_never_knew_about_stephen_colbert_partner/

Siceloff, Steven. "COLBERT Ready for Serious Exercise." NASA, May 5, 2009. https://www.nasa.gov/mission_pages/station/behindscenes/colberttreadmill.html

Spitznagel, Eric. "Stephen Colbert." *Playboy*, October 27, 2012. http://www.ericspitznagel.com/playboy/stephen-colbert-playboy-interview/

"Stephen Colbert." *Northwestern*, n.d. http://www.northwestern.edu/about/our-people/stephen-colbert.html

"Stephen Colbert Presents $171,525 to the 'Yellow Ribbon Fund' Charity on *The Colbert Report* for the Sales Generated by his WristStrong Bracelets." *Yahoo News*, January 24, 2008. https://www.veteransadvantage.com/va/vetnews/stephen-colbert

Swartz, Tracy. "Schwimmer, Colbert Recall Their Northwestern Performances, Bad Hair." *Chicago Tribune*, February 3, 2016. http://www.chicagotribune.com/entertainment/tv/ct-david-schwimmer-stephen-colbert-northwestern-20160203-story.html

auction (AWK-shun)—To sell to the person who bids the highest amount.

comedian (kuh-MEE-dee-un)—A person who makes a living by telling jokes and being funny.

confirmation (kon-fir-MAY-shun)—A Catholic ceremony during which a young person is officially accepted as a member of the church.

correspondent (kor-eh-SPON-dent)—A reporter who gives the news from where the action is.

improv (IM-prov)—Short for *improvisation* (im-prah-vih-ZAY-shun), a style of comedy in which people make up their answers and actions as they go.

marine biology (muh-REEN by-AH-luh-jee)—The study of creatures that live in the ocean (saltwater).

node (NOHD)—A room or section.

predicament (pree-DIH-kuh-munt)—A difficult situation.

satire (SAT-yr)—A form of storytelling that uses humor, irony, or exaggeration to criticize someone or something to make it seem silly.

PHOTO CREDITS: Cover, pp. 1, 25, 26—Neil Grabowski; pp. 4, 6—NASA.gov; p. 7—Tomas Del Caro; p. 12—Eric Frederick; pp. 15, 24—Anthony Turner; p. 16—SBlacksmith; pp. 18, 21—US Army; p. 19—David Jackmanson; p. 20—Gage Skidmore; p. 22—Dion Hinchcliffe. All other photos—public domain. Every measure has been taken to find all copyright holders of material used in this book. In the event any mistakes or omissions have happened within, attempts to correct them will be made in future editions of the book.